SECRETS

3 Monologues for Women
3 Monologues for Men

Stephen Baker

Running time for each monologue
10 - 15 minutes

TSL Drama

Published in Great Britain in 2019
By TSL (Drama) Publications, Rickmansworth

Copyright © 2019 Stephen Baker

ISBN / 978-1-913294-04-5

Cover photo: https://pixabay.com/illustrations/mysticism-beyond-bridge-death-666965/

https://pixabay.com/photos/paper-drilled-down-open-paper-torn-3343947/

Rights of performance

Contents

Sunbed Mike

Gail is in her early 40s, a divorcee.
She lives with her new partner Mike.

Setting

Scenes 1 & 3 : armchair
Scene 2: chair
Scene 4: wooden chair

Performance time:

12 minutes

Scene One

Lights up.

Gail sits in an armchair in her lounge.

My mother used to say to me, 'Gail always think things through, don't jump from the frying pan into the fire.' Wise words. Wise words indeed. Relationships are very tricky. We all yearn for them, and we enter into them not knowing how it will all turn out. I married late in life, I was 32. It may have been that I was panicking a bit, frightened of being left on the shelf. Which was another piece of wisdom from mother, 'don't get left on the shelf, don't be an old spinster like Auntie Elsie.'

Pause.

Anyway, I had just broken up with a guy, when I met my husband to be Geoff. It may have been on the rebound, I don't know. I had taken my car to the local garage for a slow puncture and Geoff was the mechanic. He looked quite nice in his overalls, and I could see that he looked after himself, quite muscular. We got chatting about my car etc, etc and he asked if I was single. When I said that I was he asked if we could meet for a coffee. I agreed and then we started dating.

Pause.

I was really turned on by his physique. Out of his overalls he looked great in his t-shirt which clung to his body. Very muscular. Different to my previous, who was skinny. I thought that if I found somebody totally different, then I wouldn't fall into the trap of 'jumping from the frying pan into the fire.' Geoff worked out after work at a local gym. He would come to my place later on in the evening. It wasn't long after meeting that we got engaged and then married. A bit of a whirlwind romance really.

Pause.

We bought a house together and everything was going well. We started a family, Kim was born within a year of being wed. Bringing up a young one can be very difficult and time consuming. Geoff was good with Kim, they spent a lot of time together. He would come home straight from work rather than go to the gym, so he could play with her. That's when things between us started to go a bit downhill. I noticed that he started to put weight on and he just didn't look too good on it. If I'm honest, it affected the physical side of the relationship. Well basically, he just didn't do it for me anymore.

Pause.

When you go off someone you start to notice things about them that you didn't notice before. Bad things. I had to tell him time and time again to wash his hands properly. He would just pass them quickly through a running tap. If his hands saw any soap, it was a miracle. Dirty finger nails and uncombed hair. It was just horrible. And his dress sense seemed to go. He was still buying the same waist trousers as before, but they were fitting below his now expanded stomach. Not a pretty sight. Anyway, to cut a long story short, things got worse and we parted. We divorced soon afterwards.

Pause.

I then met Mike when I joined a local gym. I thought it would be good to get fit and meet new friends. After a while I noticed this good looking guy, great physique and tanned. Boy was he tanned. We got chatting and he asked me out. We started dating. What impressed me about Mike was how well groomed he was. Always immaculately turned out whenever we went out together. I noticed that he always had a tan, even when it got to the winter. He explained that as well as working out at the gym, he also liked to use the sunbed, as he had light skin and felt that he looked better bronzed. I wasn't going to argue. I had the lot, a fit guy, with a bronze body and not a hair to be seen on his body due to 'manscaping.' What more could a girl ask for? And he also had a good job as a double glazing salesman, so had plenty of money, as an added bonus.

Pause.

It was a couple of years of courting before we got married. I didn't want to rush into anything and I wanted Kim to get to know him. Kim is okay with everything, she sees her dad on a weekend and spends the rest of the time with us. And we get the whole weekend together. Works all round really.

Pause.

After seeing Geoff going downhill, I must admit I was a bit weary of history repeating itself. But it didn't. He remained attentive to himself, and he didn't neglect me. He was very attentive. But I have never been out with a man before who takes longer to get ready to go out than I do. He spends a fortune on clothing, shoes and aftershave. He smells nice, unlike Geoff who often smelt of oil. Yes, he's a bit vain. But he's a good looking man who likes to make the best of himself. And to do that he has to have the products, the moisturising cream, the lotion and so on. Men's grooming kits are very extensive. He has a lot of combs and brushes for his hair. Anyway, he has a lot of stuff, so the bathroom cabinet has a lot more of his things in it than mine. So what, is what I say. And because he's a professional guy, he's in a suit first thing in the morning, not a pair of scruffy jeans and a t-shirt like Geoff.

Pause.

Whilst we were out one evening we bumped into some of his work mates. They'd had a few too many, I think. Anyway, they came over and were in a very joking manner. They let on that Mike's nickname at work was 'Sunbed Mike,' which I found very amusing, Mike didn't. Anyway, it didn't spoil the night. We moved on somewhere else, had a nice meal and ended the night in a wine bar. Mike was very careful not to eat a lot, small portions and no deserts. I don't mind that. Geoff used to shovel a giant helping of a main meal down his gullet like there was no tomorrow.

Pause.

As far as I'm concerned, I have met the man of my dreams. I just wish I had met him a lot sooner. And I don't care if his nick-name's 'Sunbed Mike.' I would sooner climb into bed with a bronzed 'Adonis' than a fat lump smelling of oil anytime.

Fades

Scene Two

Lights up.

Gail sits in a bedside chair in a hotel room. She is wearing shorts and a vest.

Well, here we are in sunny Madeira. This is our little winter sun holiday. Mike's just gone to the gym in the hotel. Likes to keep himself in shape even when we're on holiday. I'm not complaining. He looks great as usual. It was never more telling just how good he looks with all the effort he puts into his appearance than when we got to the hotel on the first day. We got changed into our beach wear. I've got my top and shorts on. Mike appears in his tight fitting blue shorts with his slim fit t-shirt, and of course he is completely bronzed. When he goes on the sunbed he goes completely naked, no white lines around the nether regions. And his manscaping means that he has no hair on his body. And I have to say I'm with him on that one. Geoff was very hairy. I asked him to have a body shave and wax once and he nearly went into meltdown. I think he thought it was a threat to his manliness.

Pause.

So there we are, stood in the foyer of the hotel with all the other Brits. Well, if you'd seen some of the sights: short, fat blokes with pale complexions in Hawaii shirts with shorts down to their knees and white socks, and wait for it – Jesus sandals. What a sight that was. And there's Mike looking like he's on the catwalk. Boy did I feel great walking out of that hotel with him, and boy did I feel sorry for the wives and girlfriends of the blokes in the Hawaii shirts. I can tell you he got some looks from the women. Well, he's with me darling, I thought.

Pause.

The three of us have been spending some time together. However, Mike does like to have his own space. And I'm not one of these women that demands that every minute of the day is spent together. He liked to go out on his own particularly on an evening. He said he just likes to go for a walk and clear his head, relax basically. Well why not? He works hard Monday to Friday. He deserves to 'chill out' whilst on holiday. He gives me some money and tells me to take Kim somewhere. There's always things for children to do. Lots of games' areas in the hotel, swimming pool ...

Pause.

When me and Kim were out walking one time we did see Mike talking to some local men. They all seemed to be getting on laughing and joking. Mike speaks fluent Spanish, and other languages, French and German actually. That's something else about him that is so appealing, he is very well travelled. His passport is amazing. It puts mine to shame. He's been all over the world. I had one trip abroad with Geoff, because of his fear of flying. I managed to talk him into a trip to Paris. He insisted on going by Eurostar. It was hardly the holiday of a lifetime really. I'd been to France many times before. And he made no attempt to learn the lingo. He would just pop into a shop and point at what he wanted and speak English very slowly. It was rather embarrassing.

Pause.

The way Mike was conversing with these men, it was something to admire. I could tell they were locals because of the way they were dressed. Let's just say they weren't wearing Hawaii shirts. Mike seemed to be enjoying himself and I didn't want to interrupt him, whilst he was in full swing. They all seemed a lot younger than him and they seemed very interested in what he was saying. He has a way with words. He was probably selling them double glazing. That'll be a first round here where it is permanently hot. He does know how to hold court. He didn't see us, so we just walked on. We were going to the amusements. Kim loves playing on all the machines in there. Mike gave us plenty of money with the simple instruction, 'make sure Kim has a great time.' Well she is.

Pause.

We have been getting back to the hotel around about 9ish local time. Mike would usually come back about 10, he will always shower before getting into bed. Which is good because the heat can make you a bit sweaty. What I have noticed is he hasn't been too interested in sex since we've been here. He said that he feels a bit awkward with Kim being in the next bedroom and the walls being quite thin. He also said that the heat has made him a little tired. So, basically when he's come to bed we might have a bit of a cuddle and that's it really. I'm sure things will pick up when we get back home.

Pause.

I've got time to myself. Kim's gone off to do some organised events that the hotel has laid on, and Mike has gone off for another walk. He said that he wants to go for a long walk to get rid of some of the extra calories he's put on. The meals at the hotel have been a bit more elaborate than we are used to. Me? I can eat anything without putting weight on. And Kim eats like a horse. Poor Mike, always worries about his weight. Always gets weighed first thing in a morning. He says that he must weigh no more than eleven and a half stone. Anyway, this morning he gets on the scales and he's put on three pounds. Well, what a commotion! Anyone would think a doctor had said he was morbidly obese. He was stamping about, I could hear him cursing. To be honest, I was glad he went off on his own. He was in a right strop with himself. It gives me a bit of 'me' time. It's hard being a mother and a wife. Dealing with the needs of other people. Kim's going through that funny stage, she's eleven; not really a child anymore but not a teenager. Well not yet anyway. We've got that delight to come. She can be a bit of a madam.

Pause.

Then there's Mike, with his little tantrums every now and again. Always seeking perfection in his appearance. I've tried to tell him that no one is perfect, and nobody loves everything about themselves. It just falls on deaf ears. I've noticed he's always glancing in the mirror even when we're out. And his trips to the bathroom can last forever.

Pause.

Anyway, I am determined to enjoy this holiday. Kim's having the time of her life, I'm getting some time on my own, which I am not used to, and Mike is getting some free time to do what he wants. It might not be what everyone else is doing, but it works for us.

Pause.

Well anyway, I'm going off to the pool (*Gets up from the chair*). I'm going to lay on a sun lounger, drink pina colada and read my book.

Fades

Scene Three

Lights up.

Gail sits in an armchair in her lounge.

Well, we've all come back refreshed from the holiday. Kim's gone back to school with a lovely tan and a lot of things to tell her school friends. Mike's gone back to work. I feel as if I've been able to recharge my batteries again. It's hard being a stay at home mum, doing the daily chores, etc. But anyway Mike is back at work earning good money that pays for these trips away on a regular basis. We've already booked to go away again at Easter. We're going to San Francisco. Mike's been many times. I've seen his passport, he's been a regular visitor for a number of years. For me and Kim it will be our first time.

Pause.

Mike hasn't been his usual self since we've been back. A bit moody. I put it down to the weight gain. Our sex life hasn't really got back into swing since we got back. But give it time. I'm sure everything will be fine. I've got a few tricks up my sleeve. Let's just say I've been lingerie shopping. I feel that as soon as he gets back into training and loses the few extra pounds that he put on from the holiday he'll be back to his old self again. I think the weight gain affected his confidence a bit.

Pause.

Anyway, he's told me he'll be in late tonight as he is going straight to the gym from work. I must admit he is acting rather strange and I do find it a bit disconcerting. He's become very secretive. He has taken to washing his own clothes when he comes in from the gym. No sooner has he got through the door and he is going upstairs for a shower, coming down in his night attire and throwing everything in the washer. I spoke to a good friend of mine Nicole, who felt he might be having an affair. She didn't say it nastily, but she did say that it sounds suspicious. I asked why she thought that. She said, 'because he may have perfume on his clothing and if he washes them straight away he is disposing of the evidence.'

Pause.

Well it just left me speechless. I just couldn't bear the thought of him with another woman. I must admit he did get a lot of attention from the other women on holiday. I mean when you compared him to their husbands it was hardly surprising. But to be fair, he didn't encourage it and I didn't see him flirting with any of them. But now I am very concerned. I could just confront him, but I don't know what good that would do. If he is seeing someone else, he is hardly likely to admit to it. If he is not seeing someone else then he could seriously take the huff and it could finish us. It's a real dilemma.

Pause.

I think what I am going to do is say nothing. But I am going to try and get to his washing before he has a chance to put them in himself. If there is anything incriminating with his washing, then at least I will know.

Pause.

There is a sound of a car door being slammed shut.

Here he is now. I'm going to put my plan into action.

Gets up and walks towards the door.

Fades

Scene Four

Lights up.

Gail sits in the kitchen of her home on a wooden chair.

Well what a last few days it has been. I feel as if I've been in a hurricane and have only just got out by the skin of my teeth.

Pause.

As I said I would, I put my plan into action. I brought the washing basket down from upstairs and waited near the back door where the washing machine is. He always comes through the back door via the garage. When he walked in I said, 'I'm putting a wash in, is there anything you want washing?' To which he replied, 'I have the clothes that I have on but I would rather I put them in on their own.' Well I was prepared for that response. I said that I only had a few garments and it was stupid to have two small washes when you could have one big one. I passed him his dressing gown and told him to strip there and then, as I said I wanted to get everything in and washed so that I could dry everything on the radiators. I can be very forceful when I want to be. He did as he was told. I couldn't smell anything particularly on his clothing, but I couldn't stick my nose right up to them.

Pause.

I had to act nonchalant so as not to raise suspicion. He went upstairs to get showered and I put the washer on and proceeded to get the dinner ready. I must admit as I saw the clothes going round in the washer I had a sense of relief, because I felt I was washing away my doubts. He came down all showered and we talked over dinner and basically everything went well. The three of us had a nice quiet evening. When the cycle had finished I went through and retrieved all of the items and placed them on the radiators. No problem. I then went through to the living room and enjoyed the rest of the evening. I felt relieved in a way.

Pause.

In the morning after seeing Mike off to work and Kim off to school, I set about my chores. I ironed mine and Mike's clothes. I then went to get my woollens that I had put to one side which needed washing obviously on a woollen wash. I took them downstairs, opened the washing machine door to put them in. I stopped in my tracks, because there in the drum was a piece of paper. It must have been in one of the items that I had put in the washing machine the previous night. I knew it wasn't from any of my items. I slowly retrieved it. It was folded in two. Because it had been through the wash it was crumpled. I opened it very delicately. There was some writing on it, which I could just about make out when I shone a torch on it. It read, 'This is my new address,' and gave an address in the next town; and it was signed off, 'with love Alex. X. I was dumbfounded. I just couldn't get my breath.

Pause.

When I had composed myself, I rang Nicole and told her. She said, 'I knew he was up to something.' I asked her what she thought I should do. She said that I should confront the woman in her home and let her husband know what has been going on; and then tackle Mike with the evidence. Then she offered to come round in her car and take me to the address.

Pause.

So she came round about an hour later. We set off to the address. My heart was pumping. We found the address and pulled up outside. A car was in the drive and I noticed the personalised number plate: ALEX, so we knew that we had the right address. We both marched down the drive. I walked over to the front door and rang the doorbell. The door slowly opened and a young man stood there. I said, 'Your wife Alex is having an affair with my husband.' There was a pause, and he responded, 'I am not married.' I pointed to the car and said, 'so who is Alex?' He said, 'I am.'

Fades

Always a Blue

Sheila is in her late 50s.
She lives alone in the house she used to share with her husband,
Paul.

Setting

Scenes 1, 2, 3: armchair

Performance time:

10 minutes

Scene One

Lights up.

Sheila sits in an armchair in the lounge of her home. She is casually dressed.

Just a few days to go to the big derby day. Everton versus Liverpool. I know Paul will be there. Always has a season pass. He'll be in his usual place in the Gwladys Street Stand.

Pause.

It's always been Everton with Paul. The first time I ever met him he was dressed in his Everton shirt. We were both fifteen and it was 1976. The hottest summer on record. And it was extra hot for me, if you know what I mean.

Pause.

Our respective schools had arranged for the fourth formers to have a reward for all the hard work we had done, and I think to give us a break before the hard slog of the final year, O levels and all that. Our school was in Norwich, Newbridge All Girls Comprehensive. We were all excited when we were told we were going to Sheffield Ice Arena at the end of term.

Pause.

We were even more excited when we got there and discovered that other schools from all over the country were there as well. I was just getting my boots on when my best friend Tina Dimmock came running into the dressing room and announced that she was being chatted up by a lad from Liverpool. 'There's loads of um,' she said in her broad Norfolk accent, 'and they're all Liverpool fans.'

Pause.

Coming from Norwich I wasn't much interested in football. Some of the boys I knew down the street supported Liverpool. I think a couple of boys in the next street went to Carrow Road on a Saturday to see Norwich City. A bit nerdy they were. Not my type at all, and not anyone's type really, never saw them with girls.

Pause.

Anyway, I quickly got my boots on and headed to the arena to see what all the fuss was about. And there on the ice were the Liverpool lads and girls. It was a sea of red shirts except for one blue shirt. That was Paul. He was the one holding onto the rail. I was holding onto the rail as well and we sort of met half way. I could tell he was quite unlike his school friends who immediately hit on everyone from our school.

Pause.

Paul just had the most amazing smile. A smile I was to get to know very well. It melted my heart. He had a 'little boy lost' look about him. We both ended up on the floor hanging onto each other for dear life. (*She laughs.*) Neither one of us could get the hang of skating if our lives depended on it. We gave up after a few attempts and ended up in the café area, drinking Coke.

Pause.

Sometimes you just know when you have met someone that you are going to get on with. And football didn't really come into the conversation. But I did comment that he stood out a little from his friends. I wasn't just referring to his Everton shirt. He just had something. The smile, the look, and those eyes. We knew we wanted to see each other again. This was a time before mobiles and social media. We exchanged landline telephone numbers. That was how it was done in those days. And it was up to the boy to get in touch.

Pause.

I went home thinking he won't get in touch. When he gets back to Liverpool he'll forget all about the girl from Norwich. But how wrong I was. He rang every night until I agreed to see him again. I persuaded my parents to let me go by train back to Sheffield and we would spend the day together. It was always a Sunday, Saturday was taken up with watching Everton, home and away.

Pause.

Apparently they weren't very good in the 70s. When I told my cousin Keith who Paul supported, he said, 'You mean Everton 0.' I could always gauge what mood Paul would be in when we met the day after a game. I would watch the results come through on the Saturday so I could tell what mood he would be in. It was usually sad, I have to say. Especially when they had played Liverpool.

Pause.

I wasn't to know just what part in our lives Everton was going to play. In the end it was massive. We carried on seeing each other after we left school and inevitably got engaged. The marriage was arranged in June 1979, after the football season had finished, obviously.

Pause.

Paul's family took control of the wedding day arrangements. The church they picked was actually adjacent to the ground. When we had finished with the formalities, the hymns and the vows we walked back down the aisle to the sound of the Z Car theme tune, which apparently is always played when the team runs out for the home games. It felt a crime had been committed. Maybe it was an omen. Paul's sister, Marie had already advised me to wear blue on the wedding night, as she put it: 'If you want to have a night to remember wear the team's colours.'

Pause.

Well, a girl's got to do what a girl's got to do.

Gets up and walks to the door.
Fades

Scene 2

Lights up.

Sheila sits once again in her armchair.

Yes, it was a wise choice to wear blue for our wedding night. Not sure what would have happened if I'd worn red. He'd have probably left the hotel never to be seen again. Anyway, if Paul's family got their way on our wedding day, mine got their way on our living arrangements. Paul moved in with me in my parents' home here in Norwich. Quite a common occurrence in those days. Father got him a job with him as an insurance salesman. He thrived in this role. It was the 'little boy lost look' that he still had. No one could possibly think he was pulling a fast one. He worked his way up the ladder and ended up as sales manager for the whole of North England. He was away a lot which was a problem for me but not him, he spent a lot of time at the Liverpool office, so he got to see his beloved Everton for all the home games and managed to fit in some of the away games too.

Pause.

It was difficult at first living at home and well you know (*She puts hand to side of her mouth.*), enjoying the physical side of the relationship. Things were better when we got a place of our own. I did what women do to spice things up a bit. I joined the local Ann Summers' parties, which was run by a neighbour, Claire. She remarked one evening: 'You must be the only lady who stays away from the red knickers and suspenders. They go like hot cakes round here. It's always blue with you.'

Pause.

Paul used to take me to the odd game at home. But I didn't really enjoy it. All that swearing and some of the blokes looked like they'd do something to you if you didn't jump up and down like a crazy person when they scored. Not that that happened too many times. It was a bit boring if you ask me. Then I stopped going and they had a change of fortune. Paul said that I maybe was a bit of a jinx and should stay away. They won the FA Cup then the League. I'd never seen Paul so happy. His job meant that he was away from home a lot, but the money he earned gave us a fantastic home, and a lovely car. I couldn't grumble really.

Pause.

Like lots of young couples we talked about starting a family. Paul obviously wanted eleven boys, so he could groom the next Everton team. 'We've always had a good youth team,' he said. 'I am not giving birth to eleven children,' I said. Turned out I wasn't having any. After many attempts to get pregnant, I visited a fertility clinic and we were told that I could never conceive. Paul was very understanding. I think in a way he was relieved that he wasn't the problem. It's a man thing, I think. A threat to their manhood, if they can't father kids.

Pause.

We tried all sorts of treatment but nothing worked. Life went on really. We were both upset about it. But we never let it show. Paul carried on going on his own to Everton and I would always get up early on the day of the game and iron his Everton shirt and place it neatly on the breakfast table for him. I would then get on with my chores and watch the scores as they came through later in the day so, like I had done as a smitten teenager, I could gauge what mood he was going to be in when he came home.

Pause.

When new technology came in we communicated by text. He would give me running commentary on a game. Texting me the score followed by the appropriate emoji, a happy face for an Everton goal and a sad one for the opposition. Double emojis when they played Liverpool.

Pause.

I really did become a football widow. When Sky came in with their sport channel we ended up with an enormous television stuck on the wall and a sports package to boot. Some big wig at a university said that you can always tell an intellectual, their book shelf is always bigger than their television. All I can say is that I'm glad he never came to our house!

Pause.

Still the big television was handy for me. When he went to matches I had all day to myself to watch whatever I wanted. I could watch *Coronation Street* on the big screen. It was like being at the pictures. I would sit there with my cuppa tea watching repeat after repeat. It reminded me a bit of going to pictures with Paul when we first met. We were regulars at the cinemas in Sheffield when we use to meet there. My mother and father had stipulated that we were not to go in a pub. So the cinema was the only place that we could go. My mother would always cross examine me when I got home, as to what film he had taken me to see. I had to give every detail before I was allowed to go to bed.

Pause.

It's strange how life can go full circle. Now it's me asking all the questions. As soon as Paul walked through the door I was asking him about what he had been up to whilst he was away. I wanted to know everything, he had to account for each day and especially the night. I sat there weekend after weekend watching various soaps. I always thought of Paul and wondered if he would ever stray. Of course he always swore blind that I was the only one for him. Blah, blah, blah. One time he said that you can always trust a guy who stays with his football team through thick and thin, he will stay loyal to his woman, through thick and thin.

Pause.

The television was some consolation for me, it gave me such satisfaction watching all those soaps, uninterrupted. Paul doesn't like soaps. The television only serves one purpose for him – football. Little did I know that that television which was giving me so much enjoyment was to give me so much pain.

Fades

Scene 3

Lights up.

Sheila sits in her armchair casually dressed.

We had all the material things that any couple could wish for. It was just we didn't see as much of each other as I would have liked. Always a couple of holidays abroad, and as we did not have any children we could go away at Christmas.

Pause.

We tried IVF treatment but it was no use, and we gave up after a year or two. We talked about adoption, but Paul was never keen. I always felt that he didn't want anyone else's children, he wanted the real McCoy. He wanted to raise his own blood, a boy, who would one day don the blue shirt, and run out of the Goodison Park tunnel to the tune of Z Cars.

Pause.

I have to say even with all the material things we had I often felt lonely. We'd talk on the phone and even Skyped each other occasionally. Even after all these years he still looked like that young boy clinging on for dear life on the bar at the skating rink. I think it was his vulnerability that attracted me to him. He wasn't cocky like his school friends. It wasn't just his football club support that set him aside from the rest.

Pause.

Anyway, I became the dutiful wife. Never complained. Always had his Everton shirt neatly ironed for him every game. I made sure for the midweek games one was packed in his suitcase, given that he was generally working away Monday to Friday.

Pause.

I took solace in the television and the various new channels that were available. I could watch re-runs of old television programmes. When Paul was away I watched old episodes of my favourite programme, *Coronation Street*. It was on Saturday 14 April 2012, a date etched in my memory that I consoled myself with *Coronation Street*. How could I recall the exact date? You may very well ask. Well, I'll tell you.

Pause.

It was the day of the FA Cup semi-final, and Everton were in it; and it wasn't any old semi-final. They were playing Liverpool. Paul had arrived home from working away on the Friday evening all exited. He could barely console himself on the evening. Fussing over which Everton shirt he should wear. He had twenty to choose from. I thought it was women who had the most clothes. Always visiting the club shop when he was away working. Had to have the latest shirt, sweatshirt or jacket. So whatever the weather he was kitted out. Then we had to look at which garment might be luckier than the others.

Pause.

He finally decided on the blue replica shirt for that season. How he knows the difference beats me. Anyway, as always I ironed his shirt and placed it in the usual place for the morning. We retired to bed early, as you do when you haven't seen each other for a week. Little did I know that it was the last time that we would be together.

I waved him off early in the morning and went about my day wondering what mood he would be in when he came home on the evening. But he wasn't coming home.

Pause.

I sat down in the afternoon to watch my re-runs of *Coronation Street*. It was the episodes around Ken and Deidre's relationship problems. I really felt for Ken when she told him she wanted a divorce. I kept in touch with the football as it was screened live, so I would keep switching over to see how it was going. I also had my mobile next to me. It wasn't long before it pinged and there were two smiling emojis and a message 1-0.

Pause.

I turned over straight away to see what was happening. The cameras were zooming into the crowd. Everton fans were celebrating by jumping up and down. Then the camera started to pick out fans and beam them onto the screen. It always makes me laugh when they do this. The unsuspecting fans suddenly realise they are on the big screen and nudge each other, then they all look startled, then they go crazy, waving to everyone back home.

Pause.

The camera zoomed in on a family, a man, woman and two young boys. The woman had her head on the shoulder of the man. The man was Paul. They looked so good together. Then they realised they were on the big screen. She looked and smiled and nudged the two boys. They waved franticly at the screen. She nudged her partner, he looked like a rabbit caught in a car's headlights. It was a look of shear fear. The look I first saw on his face all those years ago in the ice arena.

Pause.

Needless to say I didn't get any further text messages from him to tell me that Liverpool had scored two goals and won the match. When I tried to contact him he had turned his mobile off.

Pause.

I rang his sister, Marie. She told me that he wasn't coming home again. Apparently he had met this woman when he was away at work around the time that we were informed that I could never have children. He entered into a relationship with her and she gave him what he craved for – children; two boys.

Pause.

All this time he was leading a double life. I felt totally alone.

Pause.

Well I can't sit here feeling sorry for myself. Everton are playing at home tomorrow. I have a kit to iron. Think I'll put the sweat-shirt out for him, it could be cold tomorrow.

Gets up and walks to the door.

The tune of Z Cars plays.

Fades

Hell Hath No Fury ...

Gwen is in her late 20s.
She lives with her husband, Peter and daughter Rosie in the
family home.

Setting

Scenes 1 and 2: armchair
Scenes 3 and 4: wooden stool

Performance time:

15 minutes

Scene One

Lights up.

Gwen sits alone in an armchair in the lounge.

I married Peter when I was very young, just turned 21. I met him on a girl's night out. We were doing a bit of a pub crawl and anyway one of the crowd suggested we went to this particular wine bar which was a bit of a favourite with solicitors. Profes-sional people. We were all office workers, not factory girls, or anything like that; before anyone starts thinking 'punching above your weight' or 'gold digger.' We were just out for a bit of fun. Not particularly wanting to meet anybody.

Pause.

Anyway, I got talking to Peter. Not my usual type. He was a bit more sophisticated than the ones I generally ended up with. He was charm personified. Turned out he was a divorce lawyer. It came into the discussion with his colleagues that he was one of the best. Highly sought by those wanting out of their marriage and not wanting to be left penniless. A real high achiever. Had ambitions to have his own law firm.

Pause.

I suppose I was in awe of him. He was nothing like any guy I had ever known before. He seemed too good to be true really. He had a successful career, was extremely good looking and had the physique no girl could resist. And charm. He could charm the birds out of the trees.

Pause.

When he asked to see me again I couldn't say no. For the first date he took me to a fancy restaurant and gave me flowers. I was well impressed. He picked me up at home in his flash car and opened the door for me. A true gentleman. I thought that maybe he was too good to be true. Maybe he was just out of my league, and when he found someone on his intellectual and social level he would be off.

Pause.

After a short romance he proposed, and of course it was the proper way. He got down on one knee when we were at a posh restaurant. I got the ring given to me there and then, and then we were serenaded by a violinist for the rest of the night. Of course, he had organised all that. It was so romantic. What else could a girl hope for?

Pause.

We were married within a year and I gave birth to Rosie two years into the marriage. All planned. We wanted to start a family almost straight away. Rosie was to be the first, we talked of having additions to the family. I went back on the pill shortly after Rosie's birth, I didn't feel up to going through another birth. I wanted to have a break from having children.

Pause.

Peter started to work late a lot. He said he was the victim of his own success. Women who were experiencing marital problems would always ask for him. He nearly always won the case, with his client keeping the marital home and generally winning custody of the children, with limited access granted for the husband. I used to feel sorry sometimes for those who lost everything; Peter could be quite ruthless at times. When I was on maternity leave I would often go to court to see him in action. I have seen men sometimes reduced to tears after a hearing.

Pause.

It crossed my mind occasionally as to what would happen to us if we had marital difficulties. But I had no reason to worry unduly. He was always good to me and was an excellent father to Rosie. We just didn't see much of him.

Pause.

If we went on work events I used to get a bit jealous when I saw the interaction between Peter and some of his female colleagues. The female staff were all legs and usually blonde. And Peter stood out from the rest of his male colleagues, they were all overweight and middle-aged blokes with thinning hair. One or two looked like Rumpole of the Bailey.

Pause.

Our sex life was reasonable. I couldn't really complain. He was never just a Saturday night guy. And there was plenty of romance in the marriage. I often had breakfast brought up to me in bed. And could he cook? He often cooked a meal that was as good as we got in the top restaurants that we frequented.

Pause.

Everyone told me how lucky I was to have found such a guy. But there has always been a nagging doubt in the back of my mind. Is he faithful?

Pause.

Peter then started to talk a lot about a new divorce lawyer to the practice, Jenny. I must admit I have been getting rather tired of hearing about Jenny's activities in court. Seems she is making rather a name for herself in the divorce courts. Anyway, the other night Peter informed me that we have been invited to yet another work function. A meal out at a restaurant followed by a dance. Formal dress required.

Pause.

Anyway, the big day arrives, and I'm done up to the nines. Dress to impress I always say. We are just sitting at the table when in walks Jenny with other female staff from the practice. A tall blonde with legs up to her armpits. You know the type.

Pause.

She spent all night staring at Peter like some besotted teenager. Then they started to play some stupid game of pass the wine. Only you passed it to the next person via your mouth, after the first person had supped a glass of wine. Yuk! And double yuk! I got a Rumpole of the Bailey lookalike who passed it onto me. I didn't even know I was playing. I passed onto Peter, who passed it onto Jenny. I was livid. She loved every minute of it.

Pause.

We had a right argument when we got home. He was banished to the spare bedroom.

Pause.

If 'Miss Legs up to her armpits' thinks she can sample what isn't hers she needs to look out.

Fades

Scene Two

Lights up.

Gwen sits in her armchair in the lounge.

Peter's out again at work. Never stops that guy. I'm lucky if I get a kiss and a goodbye, before he goes crashing out of the front door and zooming off in his car. No doubt he'll be meeting the lovely Jenny at some time during the day. Apparently, they're in competition with each other to see who can win the most cases this year. Someone has put a chart up in the office and each win is marked down. So, basically men losing everything is some sort of a game. Talk about playing with people's lives.

Pause.

Anyway, whilst 'Wonder Boy' is out fleecing his gender leaving me at home to twiddle my thumbs, I decided to do something with my time. So I volunteered through the local church to visit the elderly, as a befriender. I was assigned a recently bereaved gentleman in his seventies whose wife has just passed away and he is now living on his own. His name's Tom and he has been married twice. I have been visiting him for about three weeks now. I'm really enjoying getting to know him. I'm just there for someone to talk to really. He doesn't need help around the home, he is very independent and good on his feet, and he still drives and owns a car. He lives in a little pensioner's bungalow provided by the church, it's just round the corner from me. So it's handy.

Pause.

When I go round we get talking and he tells me everything. He's had a real active life; he'd been in the army and even served in the SAS. 'Wow,' I said, 'you should write a book.' He told me about all his exploits in the Falklands War and first Iraq War. He was invalided out of the military with a bullet wound in Iraq. He then retrained and went into IT working for the military. He's a real whiz with computers apparently. I thought I must get him to come look at ours sometime. I've told 'Wonder Boy' that I can't get on the Internet half of the time. He always says he'll get around to it one day. Of course the day never comes.

Pause.

We're encouraged to let them talk freely. So, he then started to talk about his personal life. He started to tell me about both his wives. He married young with the first, had two children, a boy and a girl, John and Jackie. He and his wife Norma divorced and then he re-married a few years later when he met a single mother, Jean. They fell in love and were married soon after. Apparently, the second marriage was difficult because of the divorce settlement. He got a bit tearful when he was telling me about losing his home and not getting custody of the children and having access issues. All sounded very familiar. I generally had a running commentary over tea about Peter's latest victory. With that satisfying smug grin when he told me how the judge had sided with him.

Pause.

Listening to Tom, I got a much better perspective on the issue of divorce than I did from listening to Peter. Tom and his new wife really struggled financially after Tom's divorce. They really had to scrimp and save to make ends meet, and he had taken on Jean's daughter, Gail, as his own. Even with the army pension and his salary from his IT job, times were hard. But he always provided. I wish Peter could have listened to Tom. He might have seen what a real man does for his family. Rosie very rarely sees him and I don't fare much better. He's always working late, and then there's the gross work functions which basically are an excuse for 'dick heads' to get drunk and become even bigger 'dick heads,' if you pardon my French.

Pause.

As you might have guessed, I'm getting rather tired of Peter and his endless work, which he thrives on 24/7. And as for Jenny, I am sick and tired of hearing about her. I was watching a day-time programme the other day entitled: *The signs to look for if your man is cheating.* And the first sign? They bring their lover's name into the conversation. Well, tick that box. I have started to keep a record of how many times in a night her name is mentioned. The record is twenty times.

Pause.

The second sign is they invite them over for tea. Well, would you believe it? He came home the other night and said that he had invited Jenny over for a meal on the Saturday because she had been moved to another office in the adjacent town, and wait for it: she had broken up with her boyfriend. So little Miss Perfect was all on her own. Oh, I am sad.

Pause.

'Well,' I said, 'as you've already invited her we'll have to go ahead with it, but I'm not cooking all day. She's your guest, I'm not cooking for her.' 'Of course dear,' he said. Oh, and the third sign that your husband is cheating is that they call out their lover's name when they're in the moment, if you know what I mean. Well, if we get to stage three someone's going to be sleeping in the spare room with a black eye, and it won't be me. The programme also said that he will become secretive if he is having an affair. And come to think of it he will often disappear into the garage for a while without saying a word. When I ask him what he has been doing he responds: 'something and nothing.'

Pause.

So the big day arrived and Peter pulled out all the stops. When he's cooked for me recently I've had a basic meal, meat and two veg. This meal had everything, a starter, a main and a desert. Fantastic! He put fancy candles out and about an hour before she arrived he disappeared into the bathroom to get ready. He was that long I thought I was going to have to send in a search party. He came out eventually done up to the nines and smelling of aftershave the like I had not smelt before. It certainly wasn't anything I had bought.

Pause.

Next thing the doorbell rings and it's madam, clutching a bottle of red. 'I'm not driving she says, so we can let our hair down.' And just waltzes in as calm as you like. Nothing for me. No flowers, which I would have thought would have been a given. She then parks herself at the table in the dining room. We started eating and she started talking and we got the lot. How cruel her boyfriend was. Well I could have cried in my soup. The night was thoroughly nauseating because when she finished her attention seeking drivel they decided they would talk 'shop.' After she'd gone, me and Peter had words. I refused to do any of the washing up and went straight to bed. The next day I was going to see Tom. At least I'd have a sensible discussion.

Pause.

So in the morning I set off to Tom's. It all went well as usual and he has offered to come to look at the computer, him being an expert and all that and given that Peter can't be bothered. So I accepted the offer. The church has never laid down any ground rules for its befrienders. We are just told to befriend and listen. They didn't stipulate it had to be at their property. He's coming first thing in the morning.

Fades

Scene Three

Lights up.

Gwen sits on a chair in the kitchen. She is dressed casually. The clock behind her shows 6.00 p.m., and a calendar shows it's July.

Well what a day it's been. Tom came round as he had promised around 10.00 a.m. Peter set off to go to work around 8.00 a.m. I didn't bother telling him that Tom was coming round. None of his business really. He takes no interest these days in anything I do anyway.

Pause.

So Tom came round and got to work in the study and had the problem fixed in no time at all. It was a problem with the router which had not been positioned correctly. And I wonder who positioned that? Oh, yes it was Peter. Anyway we got chatting again about things and he said how he appreciated having someone so caring to talk to, to share his burdens. It was the sweetest thing anyone has ever said to me. I asked him if he wanted to have a cup of coffee whilst we talked and he said he did. So off I went into the kitchen. Little did I know that the next ten minutes were to change the course of my life.

Pause.

Just as I put the kettle on, the electricity blew. Everything went off. Tom came through and said, 'Where is your control panel?' 'In the garage,' I replied. I gave him a torch although the kitchen was light because of the daylight, the garage was dark because the shutter was closed and it could only be operated by electricity. Anyway, he came back and said that a fuse had blown and asked where the spare fuses were. I said, 'as far as I know they are in a tin in the garage.' He went back in and proceeded to search with the aid of the torch. Then I heard 'ah found them, here's a tin marked fuses.' I was stood with him as he brought them down from the shelf.

Pause.

He opened the tin and we both looked gob smacked. The fuses were in the tin. But so were two other items: A mobile phone and a packet of condoms. We both just stood there for what seemed like an age. I was just unable to speak. He quietly took the fuses out and placed the tin lid back in its place. He then walked over to the control panel and replaced the fuse. He was such a gentleman. He knew what it meant and he knew that I was upset. We went back into the house and I made a cup of coffee. We started to talk about his first marriage and he informed me that he had suspected that his wife was 'playing away' but couldn't prove it, and his wife had divorced him for mental cruelty. The jealousy and the not knowing had caused him to be depressed and had affected his mood swings. This had then been used against him.

Pause.

We then got talking about my situation and I talked freely. I told him that I suspected that Peter was having an affair with a work colleague and that I felt powerless to do anything about it. Tom said, 'You need to know for certain, it was the not knowing that hurt me the most.' He then told me that he saw his wife after the divorce strolling down the high street hand in hand with the guy, who he called a friend, and had suspected was having an affair with his wife. He said the pain was unbearable. In a few minutes the roles had reversed. He then said, 'When I worked for the military as a civilian I unlocked mobile phones of suspects who were suspected of planning terrorist attacks.' He made an offer there and then to unlock the phone. I took a while to think about it, and agreed.

Pause.

He went back into the garage and recovered the phone, then disappeared into the study. After about ten minutes he called me through. He had connected a cable onto the phone and into the computer. Every message sent and received was on the screen. He left me to view. I scrolled down and read every message. It was clear that he and Jenny were having an affair, and the reason for her being transferred to another office in the next town was because they had been caught in the office storeroom at it. The managing partner had disciplined the pair of them, given them both written warnings and transferred her out of the way.

Pause.

I was shattered. I returned to the lounge where Tom was. I asked him to lock it again and return it to where he got it from. I quietly closed down the computer. I really didn't know what to do next. Tom came back in and we just hugged. Nothing else. He could see how devastated I was.

Pause.

We agreed not to discuss it with anyone. Tom then left after I informed him that I would make contact when I was ready to see him again. When he'd gone I just cried, then I sat and thought it through. I didn't see any point in confronting him as he would probably deny it, and I didn't know what his reaction would be if I informed him what we had done.

Pause.

When he came home I acted as if nothing had happened. Our relationship had deteriorated over a period of time and to be honest we weren't really talking much anyway. The physical side of the relationship had gone the same way, I suppose he had decided that rather than keep two women happy, he would just concentrate on the one.

Pause.

Anyway, as they were both to discover, I may look very fragile and gentile on the outside, but when the claws come out, it's time to take cover. I managed to keep my fury under control until I decided on a course of action – except for the towel escapade. I'm afraid it was a spur of the moment thing. We were at the beach just the two of us, Rosie had gone to her friend's birthday party. Peter had insisted on going for a swim and had gone prepared with his trunks on under his tracksuit. So he could quickly undress on the beach with no problem. However, when he came back to where I was sat – I was sitting in a deckchair with a nice book, he wraps a towel around him and asks me to hold it whilst he takes his wet trunks off and puts his underpants on. I always oblige. Only this time I became distracted by a dog running near me and I forgot I was holding the towel just as he had removed his trunks. Oh well these things happen. He was totally embarrassed, poor thing. Baring his bits in front of the whole beach. Always been a bit modest has Peter about his private parts. I'm afraid he might have been at the front of the queue when intelligence and arrogance were dished out, but me thinks he was towards the back of the queue when the male tackle was given out.

She puts her hand to the side of her mouth.

Let's just say in that department he has a lot to be modest about. The whole beach erupted into laughter. Shame that.

She gets up and walks to the door.

Fades

44

Scene 4

Lights up.

Gwen sits on a chair in the kitchen. It's three months later. The calendar reads September.

Well, it's just me and Rosie now. The spineless individual, for want of a better description, has gone, bags packed, gone for good. I have custody of Rosie, and we have the house plus a generous allowance. Didn't even have to go to court. It was just a quickie divorce, irretrievable differences and breakdown of marriage. All sorted, basically I won hands down.

Pause.

We had been checking the texts on a regular basis and printing them off for evidence. I regularly checked the tin for condoms and there was always a box in there, usually minus one or two.

Pause.

We were checking the texts when we came upon a message from Jenny to Peter: 'Did the pregnancy test this morning. Bloody hell I'm pregnant. I cannot have a baby. My career comes first'. Typical. I thought, always thinking of herself. Then they get into a discussion about what they are going to do. Peter was concerned about me finding out. That's good of him. Anyway what a surprise, she informs him that she is going to have an abortion. Over the next few days we even get to know when and where.

Pause.

Tom suggests that we travel to the clinic and get proof. I asked him how we were going to do that. He said, 'leave that to me,' so I did. So, the day comes and Peter sets off as normal to go to work. He is his usual self. I get a peck on the side of the face and off he goes, down the lane. I then hurried down to Tom's. He's waiting all prepared. He's got a surveillance camera the size of a mobile. 'The tricks of the trade,' he said. And off we went in his car, with me in the back.

Pause.

We got there a good hour before they were due. Just to make sure we got them. I saw Peter's car pulling into the car park. Tom started filming whilst I hid out of the way. He even followed them into the clinic pretending to be enquiring for his young lover. I bet that raised a few laughs. (*She lets off a wry smile.*) So he had the lot filmed and with audio.

Pause.

Tom had also been able to log into Peter's email account and obtain messages from the mobile phone company regarding the monthly bill. So when we got back to the house we had a lot of work to do. Tom had arranged for a friend of his to come and change the locks on the doors and windows. He disappeared into the study with one of Peter's business cards that he leaves around the house, with his work e-mail on it. He then called me through and I sat and looked at the screen. He had loaded up my e-mail account and had an email lined up to go to Peter's e-mail address. It had the film footage, documents of the text messages and the e-mail from the phone company, which proved he was the owner of the mobile phone.

Pause.

Tom said, 'what message do you want?' I said, 'your bags are packed on the drive, you won't be coming in the house again.' He sent it. I then sent a text message to him which read, 'You've Got Mail.' I love that film. Tom Hanks is my favourite actor.

Pause.

Tom left and I packed all Peter's things in bin bags and placed them on the drive. I then rang the school to say I was picking Rosie up at the end of the school day, and I took her out for the evening, we went for a burger and then onto the pictures. We both had a lovely time. I had never felt so relaxed. When we came back everything had gone from the drive. The next day I attended a solicitors and commenced divorce proceedings.

Pause.

You know, it's a funny thing with condoms. They are generally very reliable. But not so, when someone sticks a pin in them. *Gets up and moves towards the door.*

Fades

Graduation

Simon is in his late 50s. He is married to Lyn, they have two children, Tom and Helen. Helen has just graduated with a BA degree.

Setting

Scene 1: armchair
Scene 2: desk and chair
Scene 3: wooden chair

Performance time:

10 minutes

Scene One

Lights up.

Simon sits in an armchair in his lounge. Sipping from a wine glass.

Well, it must be the genes, that's all I can say. Two kids and both graduates. I'm sure they got their brains from me. I was always top at school. Actually, I found schoolwork easy, if I'm honest. I knew as much as the teachers, and in some cases I knew more. I left school with straight As at O level as they were known then in the 1970s. I didn't stay at school to do A levels. I wanted to get out there and start earning money. Cash and girls is what motivated me. I wanted material things and the best girls hanging on my arm when I went out around the town. I didn't want to go to university. I knew that I could get to the top with shear drive and ambition.

Pause.

And basically that's what happened. I got into sales. That's where the money is. I started working for a local car dealer. He just had a small patch, nothing fancy. It was only ever a stepping stone for me. When I started as an apprentice salesman, I worked with this old guy, Harry. I learnt the tips of the trade. The next thing I was selling cars like there was no tomorrow. No sooner were they on the forecourt, I was selling them. I was dragging them off the streets. I had the real gift of the gab. It was the same with girls, I had the patter. Selling cars or any product is the same as selling yourself to the opposite sex. I would get into the patter, and success would always follow. Confidence breeds confidence. I had loads of girls and loads of cash. But I was ambitious. I wanted to move on to bigger and better things.

Pause.

I approached one of the main car dealers in the city. I told him I was the best salesman that ever walked through his showroom door. He said, 'prove to me you can sell, and I'll hire you.' And he gave me a challenge, work for him for a day and sell and I would get a full-time job with him. I rang in sick at the other place and got to work straight away at my new job. It basically was a day interview. He already had salesmen working for him. But, they were no match for me. I sold four high end cars in the day. They managed only one car between them, which was a lower end model. No contest. I was hired.

Pause.

By the time I was twenty I was the senior salesman. I was raking it in. I also started courting. Just the one girl, Lyn. Who I am now married to and who gave me two beautiful children. I met many girls using the patter. It became a bit boring to be honest. Anyway, near the dealership there was a sandwich shop. Most of us used to pop in there for our lunch. I went in the first time and there was Lyn. I fell in love as soon as I saw her. She was gorgeous. Lovely blonde hair and an unbelievable figure. I tried the patter on her and got nowhere. Which actually made me feel good. I knew she wasn't like some of the other girls I had pulled. I knew she was different.

Pause.

Anyway, I persevered and managed to get a first date. And I was actually nervous before meeting up with her. I knew when I saw her waiting for me, that she was the one for me. Alright she didn't have my intelligence, she didn't do well at school, hence the job in the sandwich shop, but she had everything I wanted. She was reserved and was elegant.

Pause.

Everything went well with Lyn and I proposed six months into the courtship. She said, 'yes,' and we married within a year. We started a family almost straight away. Tom came first then Helen, two years later. Both excelled at school. Tom sailed through his exams and went to the local university, studied economics; came out with a First and now is a business consultant. Helen quickly followed. She wanted to be different, she has an individual streak. She wanted to study outside of the city where we live. She set her heart on going to Leeds University. She got in, studying History, and has just graduated with a First.

Pause.

Of course you have to have money to put your kids through university. Lyn gave up work when we started the family. But she didn't need to work, I was raking it in. It's been a bit difficult balancing work life and family life but I think I did okay on that scale. I was doing so well at selling cars that Tony, the owner, told me he wanted me to be the sales director of his Leeds operation. He had just opened up a dealership in Leeds and he wanted me to 'run the shop', as he put it. To kick start it all, get it all running smoothly, employ good salespeople, train them up and then come back home after about six months and become the equivalent back at base. It's a ruthless game this. He already had a sales director in post at his base, so I knew he'd be gone when I came back.

Pause.

I accepted the posting. I told Lyn that it would only be for a six month period, and that I would be home on the weekend. Every weekend. It made it a bit difficult, because she was pregnant with Tom. But, she agreed, which was a good thing because I'd already taken the job. We agreed that I would pay for a cleaner to come in and clean the house weekly and my mother would call in and help with chores etc. I thought of everything. Everything went well. But something happened whilst I was away working that I'm not proud of. But it happened and I can't change the past.

Pause.

Basically, I had a fling with one of the girls at the Leeds branch. Jill worked on the reception of the dealership. As soon as I saw her I fancied her. And, to be honest I think the feeling was mutual. We started flirting, both of us making saucy innuendoes. At first it was just that and then things went a bit further after a drinking session after work. The problem with working away is that you get very lonely. I was in digs in Leeds Monday to Thursday, I travelled back to Derby after finishing early on the Friday. After the session with Jill I wanted it to be a one night stand, but it developed into something more. I was with her most days and we just grew together really. I would spend each evening Monday to Thursday with her and then Friday to Sunday evening with Lyn. I mean when you look at it; I was spending more time with Jill than I was with my wife.

Pause.

When I went home I would get the obvious question from Lyn: 'Have you been faithful to me whilst you have been away?' I would get that question every Friday evening. I would always answer the same: 'yes dear, of course. I'm never tempted.' Then I'd kiss her on the lips and pat her little lump which was Tom. Sometimes now, it cuts me up when I think of the lies.

Fades

Scene Two

Lights up.

Simon sits in his office at the Derby dealership.

Whatever I've done is in the past. I try not to dwell on it. I just put it down to being lonely at the time. We all make mistakes, and I'm not perfect. I've got a lot to be proud of, a lovely wife, and two fantastic kids. They've done us proud. Both have graduated. In a way I feel I have lived my life through them. I was so eager to leave school and get some money that I never really thought about higher education. So I guess that Tom and Helen have achieved what I should have. Me and their mother have really supported them, and the money that I earn has really made it all possible. They never wanted for anything. We made sure they got every book they needed and had money to spend so they didn't have to work silly hours in some dead end job to make ends meet.

Pause.

Anyway, after all, the effort has all been worth it. We have our second graduation to look forward to. Tom's was here in Derby. I took the day off work and me, Lyn and Helen went along to the City Hall to see Tom get his certificate, and then we took lots of photographs outside. (*Simon smiles.*) I think I bored everyone silly at work showing them all the photographs. It was great that it was local because we got to see a lot of other people who we knew at the event. And a few of us went to a local restaurant afterwards to celebrate. Of course, it's going to be different with Helen as we are going to Leeds. I'm not worried about returning to the city. There's no chance of seeing Jill there after all this time. She left the dealership shortly after I came back to Derby.

I kept in touch with one of the salesmen there who told me that she shacked up with some bloke from Hull, of all places. Well good luck to her, that's all I can say. There's little chance of bumping into her and even if we did, nothing would come of it. She's with someone else, I went back to my wife. She knew all along that I was married with a child on the way. It wasn't as if I was leading her a merry dance and promising to leave my wife for her. She knew when I left work early on Fridays that I was going back to my wife. We had an arrangement, which was Monday to Thursday with her, Friday to Sunday with Lyn. She never complained. It gave us both a good time for the six months or so that I was in Leeds, and in her life. When we started seeing each other she had just come out of a very complicated relationship and she wanted more free time. So, when Friday came around she went out with her friends and who knows, maybe even had a few blokes in tow, I don't know. I never asked. When Monday came around I went to her flat from work, which is where all my clothes were. I booked digs through the company so as not to alert Colin the manager of what I was doing. He had strict rules as regards conduct, when I started working for him. He said, 'I don't care if you sell a punter a dodgy car, but don't mess around with any of the girls in the company.' Well actually he didn't put it as polite as that, so that's not verbatim, his lecture referred to performing a bodily function and doorstep. He was very direct was Colin. He left you in no doubt what he meant. I knew he wouldn't have approved of our little liaison. So what he didn't know wasn't going to hurt him. The only other person to know was Graeme, one of sales-men. He found out by accident when he came round to Jill's flat with some paperwork from work. He got the shock of his life when I answered the door. Jill was in the bath when he knocked. Anyway, I silenced him with the odd 'sweetener.' I put him on the executive sales, these were cars at the high end of the market, so his commission was higher than that of the other salesmen. It caused a bit of agro at first, I just had to let the others know who was boss.

Pause.

Anyway, the past is the past. Let sleeping dogs lie and all that. That was my mother's favourite saying, and never a truer word said, I might add. The day is about Helen, it's her day. Her next big day will be when I walk her down the aisle. And it will be a bloody lucky bloke who's waiting at the alter to take her hand, I can tell you. A bloody lucky bloke. And I'll be one very proud father. Even prouder than I am now. So proud of both my kids. (*He wipes away a tear.*) They say that as a parent you live your life through your kids. I think that is true, certainly for me. They've both achieved something that I never did, and that's go to university. My parents would have been as pleased as punch if I'd achieved what my two have. Anyway, they'll be there on the day, as will Lyn's parents. It's going to be a great day.

Pause.

Lyn has taken Helen out shopping for her outfit for the ceremony. It's a very expensive do, is a graduation. We've booked a table at the University campus's restaurant after the event for the eight of us. Lyn's parents have never really taken to me. I think they have always thought of me as being a bit flash. They never really had any ambition you see. He was a factory worker and she was a cook in a residential home. Lyn was an only child, the same as me. But that's where the similarities end. Lyn had no ambition, she just wanted a job and some money. I wanted everything, a career, money, the lot. It's a good job we met really. Lyn's got a lifestyle which she could never really have dreamt of, growing up on a council estate with little money to go around. When we first met she was hesitant about me meeting her parents. But anyway, it had to happen when we got serious. I was invited round for tea. So, I pulls up outside of this little terraced house on a 'sink basin' of an estate in a new sports car. You should have seen the curtains twitching from the neigh-bours. Then I gets out in my flash clothes. I only bought clothes from the finest shops in town. I say so myself, I was smart. I brought flowers for Lyn's mother. I know how to turn the charm on when I need to; I was a born salesman, a charmer.

Pause.

Anyway, the first meeting wasn't a huge success. Their cat insisted on sitting on my lap and in doing so left half its fur on my trousers in the process. They could see I was a bit uncomforta-ble with it sat on my knee. When they were all out of the room I pushed it off and it let off a scream. I was left with a mass on ginger fur on my crotch. Not what a man about town wants really. Anyway, we sat down to have a nice meal and had pleas-ant chat. Jill's father never took his eye off me. He kept talking to me about my job. I found out later from Jill, that he had bought a second hand car from the dealership and had been ripped off.

Pause.

Then of course we were no sooner married and I was working away. Her dad spoke to me about it once. He said, 'I hope you're not up to any "hanky panky," whilst you're away lad.' 'No Mr Wilson,' I would always say in my most innocent voice. The problem when you are a salesman is that you never switch off, it's a 24/7 thing. I used to bend the truth at work, every day really. So, it would just become a habit. (*Changes tone.*)'Yes sir, that is the correct mileage for the car. Yes, I know what you're thinking, the owner could hardly have used it. That's because they didn't. It belonged to a little old lady who only went to the shops in it. And when she died her daughter didn't want a "boy racer" to get his hands on it and run it into the ground. So they refused to put it in the local newspaper. They came to the only car dealership in the area with a sound reputation. That way they knew it would go to someone who would look after it.'

(*Normal voice.*) The truth was it was part exchanged for a new car by a travelling salesman, and Mike the mechanic was a dab hand at turning back the clock.

Pause.

Anyway, back to the big day. Lyn has sorted out the itinerary for the day. A very good organiser is Lyn. The graduation itself is at 3.00 p.m. I'm dropping Lyn, Helen and Tom off in the morning then I'm going to the dealership to see how things are going, and then we are meeting up around 2.00 p.m. with mine and Lyn's parents in a coffee shop. Then, the eight of us will go to the City Hall for the event. I can't wait.

Fades

Scene Three

Lights up.
Simon sits in a bed and breakfast room. He is in casual attire.
I expect you're wondering why I'm sat in a bed and breakfast. I bet you think the day was ruined by Jill making an appearance. Well, you couldn't be more wrong. The day started well. I dropped the three of them off in Leeds as planned around 10.30 a.m., this gave them time to do a bit of shopping. Mine and Lyn's parents were travelling down by train and they would be meeting up around noon and then coming later after I'd been to the dealership.

Pause.

It was when I got to the dealership that I was given some bad news, Jill had died. She passed away a couple of years ago after a short illness. Graeme, the salesman told me. I was devastated. This news changed my own personal itinerary. I was going to spend the time up until about 2.00 p.m. at the dealership, but I decided to visit the flat where we stayed together for those six months. I just drove up and parked outside. I just sat there looking up at the window that overlooked the local park. I remembered looking out onto the park and feeling so happy. That's always been the problem. I was happy with Jill, and I was happy with Lyn. It was two different worlds, and I had a foot in each. I was reminiscing about all the good times we spent together in the flat when my mobile bleeped to tell me I had a text. It was Lyn telling me that they were all in the coffee shop opposite the City Hall and could I come and join them as soon as possible. I replied that I was on my way.

Pause.

Maybe it's fatal to 'feed the past' as I did. I should maybe have followed my mother's advice about sleeping dogs and all that. I parked up and walked to the coffee shop. As soon as I walked in Lyn came over and hugged me and thanked me for everything, being a great husband and father. I was choked, given where I had just been. We went over to a large table where everyone was sat. Helen looked fantastic in her gown. I was so proud. Lyn said she would get the next round of coffees in, whilst I went to the toilet. Then I came out and sat myself down with everyone and joined in the conversation. The place was just full of graduates in their gowns and proud parents and grandparents. Lyn came back and said, 'it's waiter service in here, very posh. Someone will be serving us.'

Pause.

Little did I know as I sat there talking away to everyone that my life was about to change. Tom had got up to go to the toilet. I never really noticed, I was so engrossed in the conversation with Lyn's parents in particular. I could see out of the corner of my eye a waiter bringing the tray of coffee over. I moved slightly to allow him to place the tray on the table. When he had done this he stood up and smiled at Helen. Helen was sitting opposite me. I saw her facial expression change, and then she said. 'Dad, the waiter is the absolute image of you, and looks like Tom's twin.' Just as she said that Tom came back to the table; and as fate would have it he stood next to him. Fate juxtaposed them together. I turned round to see two young identical men. Both the same height, shaped nose and dark eyes. Their facial features were also identical. It was if Tom was looking in a mirror.

Pause.

I could feel everyone looking at me and I just didn't know what to do. I had my head down like a naughty child being scolded. I then looked up to see Lyn staring at me. She said, 'Is there anything you want to tell me?' I just couldn't answer. I looked at the waiter and Tom stood together and I just felt as if the ground from underneath me was disappearing fast. Awful feelings were surfacing, feelings of guilt for the affair, feelings of remorse for Jill, I never really got to say goodbye to her and a feeling of great sadness for the lad who never knew his real father and had lost his mother. I knew the game was up. Lyn knew what had happened, women just have a sixth sense. Helen was bewildered by everything and asked what the problem was. The waiter disappeared and things came around to some normality. But it was just an act. We all knew that we had to do the best for Helen, it was her big day. We all went through the motions, taking photographs and smiling a lot. Deep down we were all hurting. The drive back to Derby was slow and painful. I think it had finally dawned on Helen what the problem was. Nobody spoke. When we got back to the house Lyn told Helen and Tom to go to their rooms. When they had left us alone, I confessed. There was nothing else I could do. It stopped her shouting. She just said, 'so every time you came back from Leeds and I asked you if you'd been faithful, you lied.' I said, 'Yes.' She told me to leave. I went quietly upstairs and packed. Within about an hour I was out of the family home and into a bed and breakfast.

Pause.

I couldn't leave things hanging. I went back to the coffee shop in Leeds and sat drinking cups of coffee until the waiter came back out. He saw me and came over. He said, 'Are you Simon?' 'Yes, I said. He replied, 'I'm Steve, Mother told me all about you just before she died.' We talked and arranged to meet after his shift had finished. We went somewhere quiet and he told me that he was in the process of tracking me down. So the story would have come out eventually. In some way I feel a sense of relief, and in a strange way; I feel if I have gained something. My marriage is over, but I feel invigorated, a bit like when Tom and Helen were born; because really I've just become a father again.

Fades

Grannie Power

Rupert is in his early 30s and works in the City.
He is a trader with a large bank.

Setting

Scene 1: desk and chair

Scene 2: armchair

Scene 3: park bench

Performance time:

10 minutes

Scene One

Lights up.

Rupert sits behind his desk in his office. He is in a suit.

Well here I am, welcome to my world. I could say that my world was created for me when I was a child. Born with a silver spoon in my mouth, I suppose. My parents were well to do. Father was a stockbroker and mother a lawyer. They wanted me, their only child, to succeed; and you'd have to say that I have. I'm at the top of my game, raking in thousands on a monthly basis, sometimes weekly. I have all the trappings of earning such an income. Lovely wife, Maria, who is Spanish and is pregnant with our first child, a large mansion in the country and an absolute must – a four-wheel drive Land Rover. Who in my position doesn't have a Land Rover? And of course I have the connections, as I'm a member of the right clubs, the local hunting, golf, rugby, and shooting clubs, members only, naturally. We don't accept riff raff. I get to rub shoulders with the right people, there's a few Lords and Tory MPs in there and old chums from school. No 'ne'er do wells' thankfully.

Pause.

There's only one problem with all the clubs I'm a member of – a guy called Jack MacDonald, or 'Mac the Knife', as we nicknamed him at school and then university. He's my real nemesis. We hate each other with a real passion. We are members of a lot of the same clubs, but we play rugby for different clubs, which makes it interesting when we play each other. It's like World War Three. And if we can get one over on each other in business, we do; and frequently. I would say at the moment it's all tied. He's a solicitor, and not only that, works at the same law firm as Maria.

Pause.

I guess my success can be put down to hard work and breeding. My parents wanted the best for me, so I went to the best schools. When you can put down a good public school and Oxbridge on your CV you are going to get noticed, doors open, if you see what I mean. No doubt it was all a contributing factor to me working for one of the biggest trading companies in the world, raking in a vast fortune. So, you'd think I would have everything. Well, I haven't. Since leaving university there has been a void in my life. I love my wife and my children, but something is missing. Sexual excitement is what I'm looking for. To put it succinctly, I have a fetish.

Pause.

I put it down to boarding school. It's the breeding ground for fetishes. All boys together, not mixing with girls of our own age. At the school it was also acceptable for teachers and indeed prefects to cane unruly boys. Well, I was one of those boys who just couldn't keep out of mischief. Always getting ten-of-the-best. 'Mac the Knife' always made sure that I got the cane. He was a junior prefect and we took an instant dislike to each other. His hatred of me came about because of something I did to him. He was the new boy at the school and I got other boys to grab him and we put him in a barrel, and then we hit it with large chunks of wood and generally shouted a lot. It was his welcome to the school. How was I to know he was claustrophobic? After that he would take great delight in telling the senior prefects what I had done, or sometimes inventing things that I had done. He'd stand there with a stupid smirk on his face whilst I was caned. There was one female working at the school – the school nurse. I was always having to see her afterwards for cream to put on my backside. I administered it, she just issued it. Lovely woman she was, Nurse Gilbert. A very mature buxom woman. I was infatuated with her. I used to think about her all the time. And of course, as a teenager, those feelings needed an outlet, and when one doesn't have privacy, if you've ever been in a boys' dormitory, you'll know what I mean, frustration ensued.

Pause.

Anyway, suffice to say that when I eventually got home I spent a lot of time in the bathroom. I was a very shy teenager. When I got to university everything exploded. Basically, I was at it with everyone. Female, I might hasten to add. Got the odd dose of one or two things, nothing too serious. And then I met Maria, who started university when I was in my last year. I studied the Classics, she was studying law. It was love at first sight. We married soon after she graduated. I was already working in the City. As soon as she graduated she joined a top law firm in London and the rest is history.

Pause.

The physical side of our relationship is only okay. Marking it out of 10, I would be pushed to give it a six. Maria is one of those 'only with the lights out' kind of women. She hadn't really known many men before I came along. How she didn't hear about my antics at university I will never know. I was practically a legend on campus. I got the rash to prove it. It went with the territory. Anyway, basically I am not meeting my needs with Maria. So, rather than feel totally frustrated most of the time and not wanting to cause any problems between me and Maria, I've decided to do something about it. No, I haven't decided to see a shrink on Harley Street. I'm not paying mega bucks for some therapist to tell me my fetish comes from my experiences at boarding school. Money for old rope if you ask me. And besides I'll probably know the guy, with all the clubs I'm a member of. No, I've decided to visit a dominatrix. I found someone advertising in the local newspaper. The advertisement said:

'strict mistress seeks naughty boys for correction and punishment.' Anyway, I rang the number and spoke directly to her.

Pause.

Of course, I wanted to know that discretion was assured. 'Of course it is darling,' she said. We agreed a fee, which was reasonable, £250.00 per hour. She gave me her address, which is in Soho. Well it would be, wouldn't it? And she said she'll fit in around my work and other commitments. Very reasonable, all round really. Sounds like someone I can do business with. I'll only visit once a week for about a couple of hours. My pay varies so much Maria will never know, and she's used to me working late and coming in at all hours. I can't see what the problem could be. It's a win, win all round.

Pause.

We discussed what I wanted. I said I liked humiliation by corporal punishment. I told her it wasn't the physical pain I liked, but the humiliation. I stressed that I didn't want to be marked on the backside. I can always get round marks on the arms and legs by blaming it on the last rugger match, if Maria asks. But I wouldn't be able to explain thrash lines on my buttocks. She had an answer for that, she has special padded trousers, and she has uniforms in all sizes. It was all a bit like ordering a pizza. Anyway, I've made an appointment for 5.30 tonight. I can't wait. I'm getting all excited. Well, I must dash, the Head Mistress is waiting. Don't want to get detention on my first day at school.

He gets up and walks towards the door.

Fades

Scene Two

Lights up.

Rupert sits in an armchair at one of his clubs. He is dressed smartly and is wearing a cravat. He has a wine glass in his hand.

Well, I visited Miss Francis as she likes to be called. She was a lot older than I thought, but that made it even better. I'd say she was in her 60s. When I got there, there was a school uniform waiting for me. She was wearing a smart outfit like she was a school head teacher. She even had an office with a name plate on it. I had to sit outside on a chair and wait to be called. After about 10 minutes the door opened and she just stood there looking at me. Then she said, 'Right Rupert, who's been a naughty boy then?' I responded candidly, 'Me, Miss Francis.' She said, 'According to Miss Dawson she caught you peeing on the new school carpet in the dormitory. Well I'm very disappointed and I'm going to have to punish you.' 'Yes, Miss Francis,' I said. Then she grabbed me by the arm and pulled me towards her. She bent me over her table and thrashed me with her cane. Then she made me stand in the corner of her office facing the wall. I moved my head to a side once without her permission and she grabbed me again and put me over her knee and gave me ten of the best with her hand. Lovely! Then towards the end of my session she made me get down on my hands and knees and polish her shoes, whilst she still had them on. I touched her nylons with the brush and received a cane right across the buttocks. Fantastic! And then just to finish things off nicely for the session, she made me stand on a chair and look in a mirror. She then berated me for not wearing my school uniform correctly. Totally humiliating.

Pause.

I was pleased with my experience I must say. It was worth every penny of the £500. I've paid that for a bottle of wine. The way I see it, it works all round really. We don't have sex, so there's no chance of getting anything unpleasant and passing it onto Maria. I'm a bit bruised on the arms where she grabbed me. But that's okay, I play rugger, you always come off the pitch bruised after a game. Maria won't suspect a thing, everything is just fine. I couldn't be happier. I reckon I can see her probably on a weekly basis.

Pause.

She's running a business like any organisation out there in the big bad world. She's seen an opportunity and she's exploiting it. And good for her, is what I say. I'm a Capitalist and she's a Capitalist. And as long as Maria or anyone else doesn't find out, we're okay.

Pause.

This club here is a private members club. Full of all the hob nobs in society. Costs a small fortune to be a member.

He sips from his wine.

It's full of sexual deviants and the like. There's a code of conduct – don't get caught. If you get caught doing something that brings shame on the club and its members, because it's a Gentleman's Club, then you are expected to do the honourable thing and resign. You resign from here and you are basically on the slippery slope downwards. A chap loses all the contacts. This is where all the business deals get done. And it's mum's the word. You don't discuss your private life in here, nor do you discuss someone else's.

Pause.

One usually finds out that a member has been a bit naughty when one picks up the paper. Recently, there was one chap, he was arrested in Thailand in a hotel with a group of young ladies. The local police had set a 'honey trap', and the poor chap fell right into it. Right up to the brown stuff he was. He's now residing in some Thai 'Hell Hole' of a prison for the next eight years, with no chance of parole. It was only a few weeks after receiving his knighthood for services to business. Oh well, you win some, you lose some, as the saying goes.

Pause.

Anyway, it's anytime now with Maria. I've been told to keep my mobile with me at all times.

He holds up his mobile phone.

If the phone doesn't ring I'll be staying in here for most of the night. I've had a long day. Started work at 8.00 a.m. as usual. Made countless business deals, visited the Head Mistress and then came straight here. Made a few more deals with certain people. All in all, when you weigh up the incomings and the outgoings just for today, I am well ahead.

Pause.

As my father used to say to me, 'all work and no play, makes John a very dull boy.' Or something like that. The session with the Head Mistress broke the day up nicely. I had a wonderful time, and I think she did. She said that she was going to totally humiliate me, and boy did she live up to her promise. It was fantastic. And I have to say I don't have one ounce of guilt over my bit of pleasure, and I look on it as a business venture. I mean when you look at it this way, there's women working in here as waitresses, probably earning just above the minimum wage, getting by on the tips they get. And they are getting felt up all the time usually by the randy old buggers in here. It's supply and demand. I want the service and she provides it. When I was stood in the corner and looked round when I shouldn't have she was doing paperwork. She was probably filling in her tax returns. It's all above board.

Pause.

Her office is in Soho, even if I was seen in that area I can just say I was visiting a client. There are loads of businesses round there. It's a perfect arrangement. Maria will never find out. So there is no harm done. I'll get home tonight, Maria will be in bed. I'll snuggle in the other side and Bob's your uncle. What she doesn't know, won't hurt her. She'll ask, 'Have you had a good day Rupert?' And I'll say, 'The best, absolutely the best.' Then we'll both have a good night's sleep and I'll be rearing to go in the morning earning a load more dosh to maintain the lifestyle.

Pause.

Well, must dash. I've got a game of Bridge booked at 8.00 p.m. Don't want to miss that. There's no rest for the wicked.

He gets up and walks to the door.

Fades

Scene Three

Lights up.

Rupert sits on a park bench. He is casually dressed and looks tired. He has his sports bag next to him.

What a day I've just had. You wouldn't believe. I've just received a text from Maria telling me that she has been taken to the maternity hospital and has been induced. And she told me to expect to be a father before the day is out. I can't celebrate. Not after what has just happened.

Pause.

Today's Saturday; and the first fixture of the season against Dorwood Rangers Rugby Club. What's the significance of that? You may ask. Well, it's the team that 'Mac the Knife' plays for. This is the match I look forward to the most. I like to kick his arse in front of his own crowd.

Pause.

The game started as it usually does against our respective teams. Mac kept winding me up, saying things like, I hear your missus is up the duff, I reckon someone's had it in for you.' The kind of remark you expect from a moron like him. I retaliated by reminding him that at public school he was a 'fag' for one of the older boys; and I said, 'In more ways than one.' Anyway, we swapped a few punches throughout the game, as you do. It all got a bit rough. The referee warned the two of us a few times and threatened to send both of us off. Anyway, they won 28-15 just to make matters worse.

Pause.

When the game finished we shook hands. 'No hard feelings?' 'Of course not,' I said through clenched teeth. He said, 'when you all get showered and changed, we've got a real evening of entertainment for you.' This is usual really. Whoever you play, the home team always put on some entertainment for you. It's usually get in the bar, have a few bevies, sing a few songs and then the strippers come on. You all have a bit of a laugh and then you go home. Or to the maternity hospital in my case. My teammates were insistent on wetting the baby's head, whether it had come out or not. Maria had asked me to stay away from the hospital until after the birth. She just didn't want me there when she was in labour. I would have been if she had requested. But she was insistent. She said, 'go and play your game of rugby and have a few drinks.' So I have. She doesn't know what happens after the game. She would never approve.

Pause.

Anyway, we got to the bar and sure enough the entertainment was a couple of strippers. The first one came on, a nice tasty blonde. Mac had obviously had a word with her, because she made a bee line for me. Kept making gestures. Then she gets this tub of talc and starts to rub it all over her naked body, she gestures me to hold out my hands in a cup, as if she is going to pour the talc into my hands for me to rub onto her body. I duly cup my hands – and she pours the full tub of talc on my head. I felt a right idiot. All I could see was Mac laughing hysterically. Then the second and last stripper come on and she singles me out. Got me on the stage, made me look a right Charlie. Had me with my pants down to my ankles chasing her around the stage. Anyway, it amused Mac and everybody else.

Pause.

Then I was given the microphone and asked to do a turn. I like Karaoke. I sang my favourite song: *My Way*. The lyrics are so poignant as regards me, and how I live my life.

Pause.

Then Mac had something else lined up for me. Something he took great pride in doing.

He takes a deep breath.

Pause.

A large screen came down behind me. Mac stood there on the stage with a remote control in his hand and a sinister look in his eyes. He said, 'Rupert as you are about to become a father for the first time, the lads at Dorwood wanted to do something special for you. Something you will always remember.' Then on the screen came all these old school photographs. Everyone thought it was hilarious seeing me with long hair.

Pause.

I must admit I was even laughing myself. Everyone was, there were really some really embarrassing photographs of me from the rugby days. We wore short shorts in the 1980s and I had a mullet hairstyle. Mac was giving a running commentary on everything. He was really enjoying it. I must admit I was, it was like *'Rupert Harris, This is Your Life.'*

Pause.

(*He takes another deep breath.*) Then Mac started talking about my behaviour and how I was always in trouble. One of my teammates ruffled my hair and said, 'Typical! Nothing changes.' And then Mac said, 'And because Rupert was always in trouble he could generally be seen outside the head teacher's office waiting to be caned.' Then on the giant screen for all to see came the scene of me sat outside of the Head's office. Not the Head's office from my school days, the Head's office from last week. With the caption: 'Grannie Power.' The dominatrix had only uploaded my sessions with her onto the web.

Pause.

The noise was deafening with the laughter. The bar was packed with all the players from both sides and club officials. I know I said I liked being humiliated, but this was something else. I stood there speechless, and then when Miss Francis put me over her knee I could take no more. I grabbed my bag and bolted for the door.

Pause.

Rupert's mobile pings with a new message. He looks at the message.

It's from Maria, she has just given birth to a baby boy. She says, 'she loves me.' Not sure that will be the case when she returns to work after maternity leave.

Pause.

If only I hadn't 'barrelled' the new kid.

Lights fade

All's Fair in Love and War

Glen is 60. He is married to Alison, they have two children and three grandchildren. Glen works as a postman, it is the only job he has had since leaving school at 16.

Setting

Scenes 1 and 4 : wooden chair

Scenes 2 and 3: armchair

Performance time:

15 minutes

Scene One

Lights up.
Glen sits in a chair in the staff canteen.

Well here I am just turned 60 and about to celebrate 40 years married. I met Alison when I started here at the Royal Mail in 1975. I came here as a 'wet behind the ears' lad of just 16. They put me in the post room to start with. I was just running errands for the office staff; taking internal mail from one office to another. There was no e-mail then, it was all leg work. And this is a massive place. I probably walked about 10 miles a day then.

Pause.

Then when I got to be 18 I was promoted to postman; and the rest, as they say, is history. I've been doing it ever since. I've never really been ambitious to be honest. Never wanted to climb the ladder. All I ever wanted was to meet the right girl and settle down. I always dreamed of falling in love, getting married and having children. And that's exactly what happened. When I was the general 'dog's body,' (*Laughs.*) I would take the internal mail all over the building, I never knew from one day to the next which office I would be sent to. Anyway, one day I was given a bundle of mail to take to some 'big wig' on the top floor. When I got there I walked into this office and there sat typing away was the most gorgeous girl I have ever seen in my life. She smiled at me and I couldn't get the words out. It took me nearly 10 minutes to tell her that the mail was for her boss, Ken Smith. She just gently took them out of my hand and said, 'Okay, I'll see he gets them.' I was absolutely smitten.

Pause.

I just knew she was the girl for me. I couldn't stop thinking about her. I couldn't even eat the sarnies my mother had made for me. It was real love. Anyway, I worked with a guy called Harry, who was about to retire. He was a wise old chap. Always giving advice, even if you didn't want it. When I was sat staring into space at lunchtime he said, 'whoever she is, she must be worth it.' I said 'what do you mean?' He said, 'you generally wolf your sandwiches down like there's no tomorrow. You've had that piece in your hand for the last five minutes. In fact, it's in danger of going stale.' He then asked, 'Who is she? Anyone I know?' Anyway, I ended up telling him the whole story of going up to the office and being met with this vision of loveliness. 'That will be the charming Alison,' he said. Alison, I thought, she looked like an Alison. Lovely dark skin and long black hair.

Pause.

After that encounter I would rush to the mail room to see if there was any mail for Smith's office. I wasn't the only errand boy. There was old Frank who used to be a postman, but was taking it easy now and transferred to an internal job until he could retire. Problem with Frank was that he was an early riser and was super organised. He generally got the best rounds because he got into the mail room before me, and he was friends with the supervisor. Anyway, I made sure that I got there before him. I would then make sure in my pile I had Smith's mail.

Pause.

One day I plucked up the courage to ask her where she liked to go socially. She replied, 'Me and my friends like to dance, so we go to the disco in the city centre every Friday and Saturday.' Well, there was only one disco in the city centre, Scamps. Right I thought, I'll be going in there on the weekend.

Pause.

Well, I couldn't go on my own. So I asked a friend, Barry. I had known Barry since school. We were sort of friends, but not real what you would call buddies. Anyway, I thought he would be good to go with because he was good at chatting up the girls; and I remembered Alison had said 'with friends'. So my plan was to get Barry to chat to her friends whilst I got to know the lovely Alison. Well best laid plans and all that. When we got in there I spot Alison on the dance floor dancing with some guy. I just couldn't take my eyes off her. I thought well I've messed up big time. Some guy's already got off with her. She saw me and waved. My legs were like jelly. Then when the music stopped she came over with two other girls. The two friends just weren't in the same league. Anyway, she came right over and we started talking. We were getting on fine and then Barry only decided to ask her to dance. She agreed and off they went, leaving me to chat to her friends.

Pause.

Barry had an advantage over me, not only did he have the 'gift of the gab,' but he could dance. Boy, could he dance. I felt a bit angry with Barry, because I had explained to him that I wanted to get off with Alison. I waited until he went to the toilet and followed him in. We had a chat and all he would say is, 'she fancies me, she can't take her eyes of me.' I couldn't say I noticed myself. Anyway, we got back and we started chatting. I asked Alison to dance and she agreed. I thought I could blag it. I thought if I just moved my legs and arms a bit in the dark no one would notice. The dance didn't go according to plan, when we set off onto the dance floor I managed to trip over a girl's handbag that she was dancing round. The dance floor was always a bit of a hazard. The girls would put their bags on the floor in front of them so they didn't get nicked. We had a bit of a dance. Just the one. I thought that would be enough to get her hooked and distract Barry. As we were walking back I was hoping Barry was chatting up one of the other girls. He was talking to them, but the body language was a bit of a giveaway. They were quite a distance apart.

Pause.

I got a round of drinks in and as far as I was concerned it was game, set and match. There was an old saying in the disco world of the 70s: 'when the "erection section" came on.' That is the smooching bit at the end; when the DJ would put on the slow stuff so you could dance with a girl close up, if you could get a girl to smooch with you, you were in. Well I intended that me and Alison would be smooching to Barry White at the end of the evening. No problem.

Pause.

So we gets to the end of the funky stuff that I couldn't dance to. And the DJ starts with the slow stuff. And on comes Barry White singing: *Can't get enough of your love.* I was just about to make my move when Barry took Alison by the hand and took her onto the dance floor right in front of me. Talk about rubbing it in. I ended up smooching with one of her friends. Not a very nice experience if you ask me. What made it worse is that we were right next to Alison and Barry. I looked and they were actually kissing. I was livid. Then her friend, whose name I can't even remember started kissing me. Not good. The plan was heading straight out of the window. I needed to act and act quickly.

Pause.

Anyway, next thing I knew we were walking out the door. Alison arm in arm with Barry and me with her friend with her arm through mine. Not sure what happened to the other friend and nor was I bothered. We all shared a taxi and the girls got out together. I didn't ask her friend out, I just said, 'see you around.' Which basically meant: I'm not interested. Me and Barry got out together as we lived near each other. We had words, and all he kept saying was, 'she likes me, and I like her.' I asked him if he would be seeing Alison again and he said that they had arranged to meet in midweek for a drink. I was absolutely gutted. We were chalk and cheese really, me and Barry. I was always a guy looking to settle down, he was a guy looking for adventure. He was always looking to get out of the city to this or that. He said the city was 'dead' and that he would be leaving it at the first opportunity. I thought, well I hope it's soon and on his own. It would have broken my heart if he had left and took Alison with him.

Pause.

I knew I had to act and as luck would have it fate played its hand.

Fades

Scene Two

Lights up.

Glen sits in an armchair in his lounge. He is casually dressed.

Well here I am in my home. My home that I share with my lovely wife Alison. We've been together now for 44 years and have been married for 40 years. We've had our ups and downs, but what couples haven't? We were meant to be together, there's no doubt about that. Cupid definitely fired his arrow, it's just that it didn't fly necessarily in a straight line.

Pause.

If you remember I was talking about 1975 and events around me, Alison and Barry, an eternal triangle. Barry had arranged to take Alison out after the ill-fated trip to the disco. They had planned to meet at 7 p.m. The next night outside the Roxy picture house. I knew this because Alison told me at work first thing on the Monday morning. I remember feeling absolutely gutted. And if it wasn't bad enough, Alison was trying to make it a foursome with me and her friend. I was having none of it. I went home feeling totally distraught. Anyway, when I got home my mother said to me, 'that friend of yours Barry has dropped a note off for you and he wants you to give it to your work colleague Alison.' I thought, what am I, his bloody errand boy now?

Pause.

As luck would have it, Monday was my mother's bingo night, and father always took her. I was dying to look at the note that was in a sealed envelope. I was hoping that he would dump her. When my parents went out I steamed it open. It read: 'Dear

Alison, can't wait to meet you on Tuesday night, I am having to work late, and can we meet at 8 p.m. instead of 7 p.m.?' I was gutted. I resealed it and put it in my work jacket pocket. You have to remember that this is the mid-1970s, no mobiles or e-mails and not everyone had a landline. I know Barry's and Alison's family didn't. The passing of notes in courtship was quite common.

Pause.

I had time to dwell on things in the evening and then on my way to work. I decided to intervene before this relationship could get off the ground. If indeed there was ever going to be a relationship. Barry just wasn't right for Alison, he was a 'fly by night character.' He had also applied to join the RAF so would probably be leaving the city shortly, and would probably take her with him, which would mean we would never have got together. I spent the whole day wondering what to do, whether to give her the note or not. I decided on the latter, and came up with a cunning plan.

Pause.

I rushed home from work at 5.30 p.m. on the dot. I gulped down my tea and locked myself in the bathroom. I was showered and hair washed and styled in no time. I climbed on the number 55 bus and headed into town. I had a bit of 'Dutch Courage', as they say, at a pub in the town centre right near the Roxy picture house. And with military precision I set off at 7.20 p.m. to walk past the Roxy. And there was Alison stood there looking nervously at her watch. She looked fantastic. I looked at her and her at me. I said to her, 'is everything okay Alison, you look a bit upset?' She called me over and said quietly, 'I think Barry has stood me up, I want to leave here without looking stupid, I don't want anyone to know.' The Roxy was the main meeting place for dates to meet up so there were a lot of people around. I took pity on her and offered to take her away from the place. Well what else could I do?

Pause.

I suggested we went for a drink on the far side of town and she agreed. We had a really good time. Of course I was a shoulder to cry on and seen as a bit of a hero, a Sir Galahad. She looked so pleased to be with me and we just got on so well. I told her to forget Barry as he was a 'bad egg.' I offered to walk her home, which she agreed to. When we got to her gate we kissed and it was just fantastic. I told her that I really liked her and said that I would really like to see her again. She said that she didn't want to rush into anything after what had just happened but would see me at work.

Pause.

When I got home my mother was waiting for me. She said, 'that friend of yours Barry came round earlier on and saw your father. He was very upset and wants you to go and see him.' I went straight out of the door and went to his house. I nervously knocked on his door. Barry answered looking distraught, and before I could say anything he said, 'she stood me up.' I said. 'I'm really sorry mate. I gave her the note and she didn't look very pleased.' And then I said, 'and I've just been round the town with a workmate and we saw her out with a friend and two guys.' 'Birds,' he said, 'you just can't trust them.' 'No,' I said, 'you can't.' I then made an excuse that I had to be home as I needed to be up early in the morning. Which was just about the only truth I spoke all evening.

Pause.

I went to sleep anxious, but in a way pleased with my night's work. All's well that's ends well, I thought.

Pause.

The next day Alison came to see me and asked me if I wanted to go out on the weekend. I said I did and we have been together ever since. I made sure that we went to places that Barry didn't. And fate worked its hand again. Barry went off into the RAF and I passed my driving test, got a car and we went all over the place. We married in the summer of 1979 and here we are two children and three grandchildren later.

Pause.

Sometimes when cupid fires his arrow you have to have a remote control in your hand and gently guide it to its target.

Fades

Scene Three

Lights up.

Glen sits in an armchair in his lounge.

Well here I am again, Lord of the Manor, in my lovely home, our love nest. It's a basic semi in a reasonable area. The best we could do on the income I get from the Royal Mail and Alison's salary. I still work there, Alison left a while ago when we started a family. She just works part-time now in a local store down the road. It all helps. Anyway, we've been experiencing a bit of a problem with the house. It was me who noticed the cracks in the living room wall, when I started decorating.

Pause.

At first we didn't know what to do. We've always had a tree outside of our house, which was one of the attractions when we came to view. It's a lovely Oak tree. One of neighbours told us that the likelihood is its roots have grown under the bay and is lifting it up. He said, 'I would get that looked at if I was you, or your house will subside.' Alison was beside herself. She said, 'Glen you must get this sorted. Contact the council and get them to cut the tree down. It's their tree.'

Pause.

So, I rang the Highways section of the council and spoke to a chap called Davies, who told me that he would come and take a look, but said, 'residents often blame trees for cracks in their property, and it's usually ground movement.' I thought you're trying to baffle me with science mate. We'll have you down here and I'll prove to you it's the tree and it'll have to go. End of. I'm a no nonsense sort of guy.

Pause.

Anyway, the next day Davies comes as arranged. Small thin bloke with a pencil stuck behind his ear. You know the type. He looked around outside and then came indoors and looked at the cracks in the wall. 'Just as I suspected, ground upheaval.' Yes, I said and what caused the ground upheaval? 'Don't know,' he said. 'Could be anything. The council has a policy of saving trees, and that one has a tree preservation order on it.' Anyway, he reluctantly said that he would put a machine outside of our property to monitor ground movement and advised that we contact our insurance.

Pause.

I duly did. Alison has been really impressed with the way I've taken the lead on this. Even though I'm working full-time I've still taken the issue on. The insurance wanted to know everything when I contacted them in my lunch break. I barely had time to have my lunch. Then they sent a representative to have a look. I met him on site after finishing my early shift. Nice chap, anyway he checked the machine and had a good look round. I was reassured when he said, 'probably is the tree. This may take some time to resolve, but I'm sure we can get this sorted.' Great, I thought, we're getting somewhere. He asked for the details of the Highways chap and I duly give him his name and contact detail.

Pause.

To cut a long story short. After six weeks of monitoring, the two sides could not agree on the cause of the damage. Both agreed there was ground movement but disagreed on what was causing it. So an independent firm was brought in and they supplied their findings after monitoring it. They found that in all likelihood the tree roots were under the house. But Davies wouldn't budge on things. Kept saying the tree had to stay, blah, blah blah. He suggested that I contact the local councillors if I was not happy. He said, council policy can only be changed by council-lors. And then he left. I've never dealt with politicians in my life. Don't even know who they are. The neighbour who advised us on the issue told me we had three Liberal Democrat councillors, didn't know who they were, but said they held a ward surgery at the local library the first Saturday in the month. Which by coin-cidence was the next Saturday.

Pause.

There's no stone left unturned with me. I marked it in my diary. Alison will be well impressed.

Fades

Scene 4

Lights up.

Glen sits in the staff lobby on a wooden chair.

I have to say the last few weeks have been the worst time of my life. I went to the local library as I had arranged. I saw the sign which read: 'Your local councillors are here to help.' I thought, well that's reassuring. Then I thought hang on a minute, Liberal Democrats, the neighbour said, I hope they're not 'tree huggers.' I want the tree preservation order removed and the tree felled. Not some middle aged hippy breaking down in front of me and weeping for the tree, citing 'trees have feelings you know.' If that happens, I'll be saying 'and do you want to live in a house that's subsiding mate?'

Pause.

I was invited to sit down by a council officer and fill in a form which detailed my issue. Nothing difficult there. Then, the form was taken away for the councillors to view before I was called to speak to one of them. Next thing I heard 'Mr Kirk, Councillor Rogers will see you now.' I walked towards this room and opened the door. Well, you could have knocked me down with a feather. Councillor Rogers is only Barry!

Pause.

'Glen,' he said, 'it's great to see you. I see you've been having a little trouble with a tree. I'm sure we can soon get this resolved. I might have to go before the planning committee and ask for the tree preservation order to be removed.' He then puts the completed form in his briefcase. It's got our address on. He then starts asking me about life etc. Are you married, kids, grandkids?

That sort of thing. I tried to keep it as brief as possible. Didn't want to set the hare racing. 'And yourself?' I asked hesitantly. 'Just got divorced,' he said. Apparently he'd been in the RAF for a number of years, married a girl in Lincoln and lived there from when he moved away to last year. He was bored and became active in the local community. Then the Liberal Democrats noticed him and talked him into standing for them in the local election. He won and is there for the next four years. Great, I thought. A blast from the past. That's all I need.

Pause.

I made an excuse and left the surgery. I thought well, he'll maybe write a few letters and keep us informed; and he only has my details so all letters will be addressed to me. I'll keep it all in hand. When I got home, I just told Alison that I had seen the local councillor and everything was in hand, and not to worry.

Pause.

Then, on the Monday evening we sat in the lounge watching television, it was around 7.00 p.m. when there was a knock on the door. Alison went to answer it. I could hear chatter, I just assumed it was one of the neighbours or one her friends just popped round. Next thing I know there's Barry stood in the doorway. Alison then appears, 'you never said it was Barry, who you saw at the council surgery,' she said. 'Oh I said, it must have slipped my mind.' I said. 'I always make home visits when it's a serious issue,' he said, 'and I was in the area. So here I am.'

Pause.

I felt like an arrow had just landed straight into my chest. He then starts to look at the damage to the wall. 'You need to look outside Barry,' I said, thinking I'll get him out of harm's way. 'Don't need to,' he said. 'I've already had a look outside'. He only stayed for an hour and a half. I was bursting to go to the loo, but couldn't because I couldn't leave them together. He kept saying, 'I just can't believe you guys got together.'

Pause.

Finally, he left when I dropped it into the conversation that I had to be up early for the early shift. But not before leaving his calling card with Alison. I couldn't do anything about it, it all happened in an instance. I couldn't make a fuss about her having the card, because it would alert her suspicions. You know what women are like. So, I had to play it casually. I said, 'It's nice to see Barry again, after all this time. Good to see him doing well for himself.' Inside, I was worried sick.

Pause.

I went to bed early but was unable to sleep. I was tossing and turning all night. I kept Alison awake, which put her in a bad mood. I got up the usual time for the early shift, 5.00 a.m. Alison was still awake and we had words about her lack of sleep. I crept downstairs after my shower and made myself breakfast and then slipped off to work. I was worried all day about events. I kept meaning to text Alison, but I didn't know what to say. Anyway, I decided to call in at the local florist after finishing work and I booked a table at the local restaurant for 7.30 p.m. Alison wasn't working so I knew she would be home when I got back. I thought, give her the flowers, take her out for a meal and everything forgiven. And maybe if I'm lucky, an early night but not for the kip.

Pause.

I got the flowers, booked the table and dashed home. I pulled up on the drive, and got the flowers in hand. I walked through the garage and burst through the door into the kitchen, and I shouted, 'Surprise.'

Pause.

The place was empty. On the kitchen table was an envelope with my name on it. I opened it and read the note, it said, 'Gone to the Roxy with Barry. Alison.'

Fades